**pocket
cornwall**

Walking in Penwith

David Chapman

Alison Hodge

First published in 2011 by
Alison Hodge, 2 Clarence Place, Penzance,
Cornwall TR18 2QA, UK
info@alison-hodge.co.uk
www.alison-hodge.co.uk

ISBN-13 978-0-906720-76-9
British Library Cataloguing-in-Publication Data
A catalogue record for this book is available from
the British Library.

Designed and originated by
BDP – Book Development and Production,
Penzance, Cornwall

Printed in China

Title page: Land's End from Mayon Cliff

Contents

Introduction

The walks in this book are all located in West Cornwall in the district known as Penwith. In selecting them I have used the criteria that I always use for a good walk. Wherever possible they are circular walks, using paths rather than roads, and include: beautiful scenery; natural history; historical features; other interest; free parking and somewhere to stop for lunch (café, inn, or at least a beauty spot). Some of the walks haven't satisfied all of these criteria, but only where there are good reasons!

For some of these criteria, I have given each walk a 'five-star' rating. Within the text I have highlighted where to park and where you can stop for lunch. For each walk, I have provided an overview followed by specific details about the route (in italics), and the points of interest along the way. My aim has been to provide information about the historical features as well as suggesting the types of wildlife that might be seen.

The timings I have given are based on the length of time it took me to complete the walks; these do not include long periods for sitting and looking, so you might need to build in extra time. You might find that I am faster or slower than you, but you should be able to use these times as a guide to help you make plans. The distances stated are approximate; within these I have tried to make allowances for the twisting and turning nature of the paths.

The maps are intended as a visual representation of the walk; they are not a substitute for carrying a detailed map. The instructions in the walk description should be enough to get you round, but I recommend that you carry an Ordnance Survey map as well, in case you lose the route along the way. All of the walks in this book can be found on the Ordnance Survey Explorer map number 102, Land's End.

The maps show: the route in a black dashed line with arrows; roads and tracks marked in red (generally, the wider the red line the bigger the road); points of interest marked in blue; start point marked in yellow. Land is green, sea is blue, and beaches are golden; areas of houses are marked in grey-green. Each map has an approximate scale and a north line.

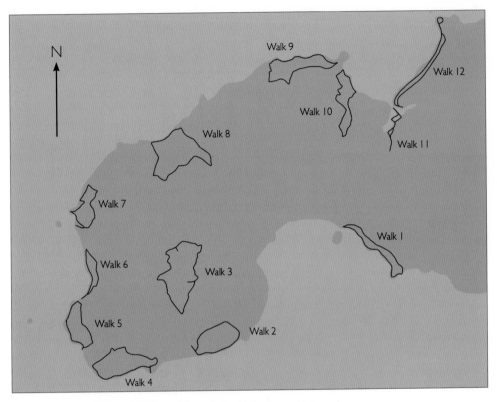

Map showing approximate locations of the walks in this book, roughly to scale

If you are interested in identifying wildlife along the way, you might wish to carry my books *Birds of Cornwall and the Isles of Scilly*, *Wildflowers of Cornwall and the Isles of Scilly*, or *Exploring the Cornish Coast*, all of which are also published by Alison Hodge in the Pocket Cornwall series.

David Chapman, 2011

1 Prussia Cove to Marazion

Beauty	*****
Wildlife	****
Historical interest	****
General interest	***
Distance	12 km (7½ miles)
Time	3½ hours
Walking conditions	Very good
Timing	Begin walk on a falling tide for walk across beach at Marazion
Start and end point	Prussia Cove car-park (SW 556 282)
Get to to start point	From Penzance take A394 towards Helston. In Rosudgeon turn right on minor road signed to Prussia Cove. Follow road to very end (narrow) and park in free car-park

A view to Cudden Point from Prussia Cove

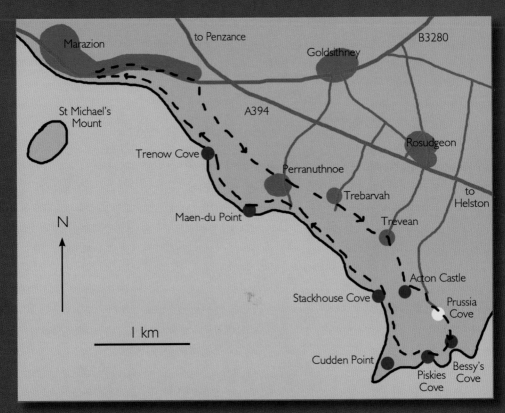

Marazion

to Penzance

B3280

Goldsithney

St Michael's
Mount

Rosudgeon

Trenow Cove

A394

Perranuthnoe

to
Helston

Trebarvah

Maen-du Point

Trevean

N

Acton Castle

Stackhouse Cove

Prussia
Cove

1 km

Cudden Point

Bessy's
Cove

Piskies
Cove

This walk along the coast provides some of the most beautiful views of Cornwall's most iconic landmark – St Michael's Mount. Having done the coastal route, you might think that the return route, along an inland path, would be a disappointment, but to see the coast from a high vantage point is in fact one of the most rewarding aspects of this circular walk.

The fishermen's hut at Prussia Cove

From the car-park, take the double-width track down towards the coast, taking the right fork signed to Perranuthnoe and Marazion.

Soon you are walking along the top of a cliff above Bessy's Cove, an idyllic little fishing cove complete with track and fishermen's shack. At low tide, note the tracks carved by years of use in the rocks on the beach. It is likely that these tracks were carved by smugglers' carts in the eighteenth and nineteenth centuries. One family in particular, the Carters, smuggled goods from here in the eighteenth century. It was they who earned the area the name of Prussia Cove, as one of the brothers was nicknamed the 'King of Prussia'. They used three coves for their illicit activities: King's Cove to the east; Bessy's Cove and Piskies Cove.

The memorial to HMS Warspite *above Bessy's Cove (left). Piskies Cove (right)*

On the first headland, you will see a wooden post. This is a memorial to HMS *Warspite*, a battleship built in 1913 which served in both World Wars. In 1947 she was to be scrapped, and was under tow heading for Wales when a storm forced her to run aground here at Prussia Cove. The men on board were all saved by the Penlee lifeboat, which put itself between the stricken ship and the rocks to carry out the rescue. Coxswain Edwin Madron was awarded the RNLI's silver medal, and Mechanic Johny Drew a bronze medal for their parts in the rescue. The post is made of wood from the *Warspite*.

This walk follows the coast path all the way to Perranuthnoe and beyond, so directional instructions can be kept to a minimum.

After Bessy's Cove is Piskies Cove; look out for the ravens and fulmars which nest here. On the headland of Little Cudden, you may notice a small wall of a ruined chapel. Here there is an inscription which reads: 'We have a building of God, an house not made with hands, eternal in the heavens; where the spirit of the Lord is there is liberty.'

Wildlife is very rich on the coast between here and Cudden Point. There is a good variety of flowers, including heather; gorse;

The view back to Cudden Point from Maen-du Point, near Perranuthnoe

dodder; spring and autumn squill; sheepsbit and devilsbit scabious; thrift and sea campion, to name but a few. An invasive plant known as Hottentot fig can be seen on the steep slopes down to the sea. Butterflies which live here include the wall brown, common blue and silver-studded blue, and many others can be seen on migration, including clouded yellow, painted lady and red admiral. Six-spot burnet moths are common in summer, and silver-y moths can be seen during spells of good weather. Out to sea there may be grey seals, basking sharks and bottlenose dolphins.

Ponies graze the National Trust land of Cudden Point sometimes during the winter, and this activity helps to stimulate the growth of wildflowers in spring and summer. From the summit of Cudden Point, the view west is astonishing and far-reaching. We can see Perranuthnoe, Marazion, St Michael's Mount, and then the distant landscape of Penzance, Newlyn, Mousehole, and as far as Tater-du lighthouse. Looking back to the east, we see the Lizard with its distinctive satellite dishes, and all the way to the most southerly point.

It isn't too far now before the coast path brings us into Perranuthnoe. 1 hr

Here there is a beach café, which is open all summer and some days in the winter. There is also a craft centre just up the road from the car-park, and toilets.

Continue along the coast path, straight across the small road by the car-park.

There is another lovely view of St Michael's Mount from Maen-du Point, and a seat from which to enjoy it. The coast path from here passes through small fields with tamarisk hedges; this delightful feathery-leaved tree was imported because it can withstand high winds and salty air.

This is great hunting ground for kestrels, and it is rare to walk here without seeing several, so keep an eye out for a bird of prey that hovers.

The footpath leads on to a small track where you turn left, and this opens out into a small car-park overlooking Trenow Cove. Don't walk down the track to the beach, but turn right on the small path just after the bench. (The beach might look tempting at low tide, but the walking gets tough around the headland.)

After passing along the cliff tops, this path eventually leads to metal steps leading down to the next beach. At the bottom of these steps, turn right, and keep to the upper edge of the beach. The proper coast path leads off the beach up a track, and is not very well signed. This path takes us up to the road leading into Marazion (turn left on this road to go down into the town), and is a bit of a detour. Much better if the tide is far enough out to take the short cut across the beach.

This beach is a good one for spotting waders. In late summer and winter, look for sanderling here. These are the small, very pale wading birds that run up and down as the waves break. Look also for ringed plover, turnstone and oystercatchers here. Keep an eye on the sandy cliffs at the back of the beach. These cliffs are eroding very quickly, and the sandy soil is an ideal place for sand martins to nest. These birds make their nests in holes near the top of the cliff.

At the far end of the beach, take the old steps up just beyond the new sea defence. We are now in Marazion. 2 hrs

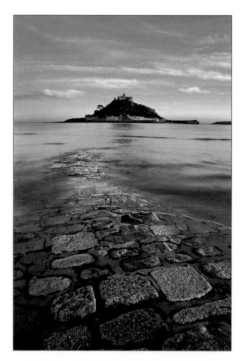

The Causeway to the Mount from Marazion

Here there are plenty of facilities and a great spot for lunch. If the tide is low, it will be possible to walk out to St Michael's Mount (the time and distance involved is not included in the details for this walk); alternatively, take one of the small boats that serve visitors in the tourist season.

From Marazion, take the road to the east, up the hill, back in the direction from which we came. You will need to walk along the road for about ½ mile. On the right you will pass the turning to the coast path (which you may have come up if you couldn't walk along the beach); then there is a cemetery; immediately after the cemetery, turn right along a footpath.

This footpath is well signed. Turn left at the junction of paths to head directly for the church tower of Perranuthnoe.

Don't forget to turn round and enjoy the views back towards St Michael's Mount.

In Perranuthnoe, you will pass Carn Perran on the left. Turn left on the metalled road, and then immediately right on a track, keeping Trevel Cottage on your left. You will come out near the Victoria Inn. Go straight across the road, on the track with Churchway Cottage on your right-hand side. 2 hrs 45 mins

Continue on this path, taking the left-hand option at the footpath junction. This leads to the farm of Trebarvah, which now has many holiday cottages. Pass straight through the farm; the footpath is well signed here. The footpath passes along the left-hand side of a large field; ignore the option of a footpath to the left. Over a stile, and follow the right-hand side of a long, thin field before emerging through a gate on to an unmetalled road.

Looking back over Perranuthnoe and the Mount from near Trebarvah

This is Trevean Farm. Keep left round the buildings, before turning right where you meet the end of a metalled road. This takes us past Acton Barns and towards Acton Castle.

Acton Castle was built in 1775 by John Stackhouse. His family home was at the Pendarves Estate near Camborne, but in 1773 he married Susanna Acton of the Acton Scott family in Shropshire. John had a passion for seaweeds, and so they built a house over-looking the sea, and the cove adjacent is known as Stackhouse Cove.

This track leads directly to the castle; the footpath we will take runs parallel to the track over the hedge to the left. Follow this path; it soon turns left up the hill, before we get to the castle. After passing through another field, the footpath brings us out on the road down to Prussia Cove. Turn right here, and soon you will be back at the car-park. 3 hrs 30 mins

2 Lamorna and St Loy

Beauty	*****
Wildlife	**
Historical interest	****
General interest	***
Distance	9 km 6 miles)
Time	3 hours
Walking conditions	Difficult stretch on coast path
Timing	Any
Start and end point	Three alternatives: lay-by at Boskenna Cross (SW 426 243) or Merry Maidens (SW 432· 245), both on B3315 Newlyn to Porthcurno; or car-park at Lamorna Cove (SW 450 243)
Get to to start point	From Newlyn take B3315 (up steep hill). Continue past left turn to Lamorna. After another mile there is a lay-by on the left for The Merry Maidens stone circle, or go a further half mile to a lay-by beside a Celtic cross at Boskenna. Alternatively, go to Lamorna Cove pay-and-display car-park

Tater-du lighthouse from Boscawen Point

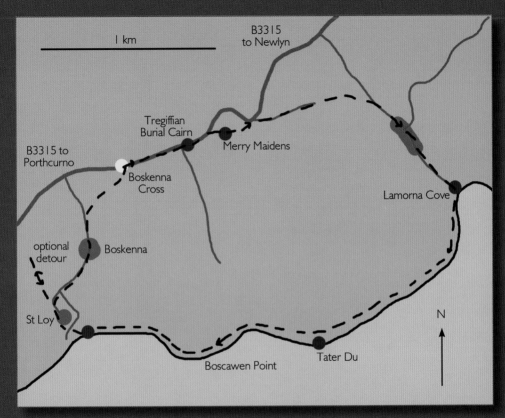

This is a very varied walk, with more than its fair share of historical features along the way. The options to stop and eat are at the pub- lic house in Lamorna, a short distance from the start of the walk, or at a café in Lamorna Cove. (The café is not open out of season.)

Tregiffian Barrow (left) is beside the B3315 at the start of this walk. The Merry Maidens Stone Circle (right) is one of the best preserved of its kind in Britain

In the lay-by at Boskenna Cross, there is an ancient Celtic cross mounted on a millstone and a cider press. It was originally in the middle of the road, but was knocked down by the army.

From the lay-by, walk along the B3315 towards Newlyn.

After about a quarter of a mile, on the verge of the road, is the site of Tregiffian Barrow. This is a late Neolithic (c. 2500 BC) chambered tomb, of which only a half is left today.

Continue another 90 m or so to the lay-by for the Merry Maidens stone circle, and turn right on to the footpath to the circle.

This stone circle is one of the best preserved in Britain. It has 19 stones, and only two of them have needed to be re-erected.

There are some buried stones to the east of the circle, which might have formed part of a processional way to the circle. The story of the Merry Maidens is that 19 maidens are said to have been turned to stone for dancing on the Sabbath.

Continue through the stone circle and to the stile over the wall. Over here, follow the line of the telegraph poles across the next field. This leads back to the B3315 at a bend, but don't go back on to this road, instead turn right on to the minor road (not the farm track).

This track passes Borah Chapel, built in 1878 but now converted into a residence. The word *borah* means 'the place of the witch'!

Continue as far as the minor road in Lamorna Valley; turn right on to this road.

The stream flowing through Lamorna valley

The valley of Lamorna has some small galleries, as it has long been popular with artists. Here there is a public house with the unusual name of 'Lamorna Wink'. The term 'wink' is thought to have been first used in times of smuggling, when if you winked at the landlord, you might be able to get some contraband liquor.

Continue down the road to Lamorna Cove.
40 mins

Here there are a beach café and toilets near the car-park.

Lamorna is probably best known for its artists, many of whom belonged to the Newlyn School. Apart from being an attractive cove, it was once used as a granite quarry, and there is still stone on the slopes of the valley.

Walk past the café and on to the coast path heading west. The first part of this path is very rocky and wet in places.

Lamorna Cove seen from the coast path (above).
A cross on the coast path near Lamorna (left)

Before you round the first headland, look out for a small cross on the left, overlooking the cove. This was erected as a memorial to a student who fell to his death here in 1873. A little further along the coast path, you will pass the small nature reserve once owned by Derek and Jeannie Tangye. The Tangyes

The boulder-strewn beach of St Loy's Cove

were writers. Derek Tangye's tales about their life at nearby Dorminack were known as the Minack Chronicles, and as a legacy they left their land for wildlife.

A little further on, we come to the Tater-du lighthouse. 1 hr 30 mins

It isn't possible to descend the steep slope to the lighthouse, but it is a notable spot as this was the last lighthouse ever built in Cornwall, in 1965, and it has never been manned. It warns of the dangers posed by the Runnel-stone Reef, just off shore. The accident that led to the construction of the light was the loss of the Spanish coaster, the *Juan Ferrer*, which went down at Boscawen Point, losing all hands, in 1963.

The stream in the valley of St Loy

Continue to Boscawen Point.

From here, there are great views back along the coast to the lighthouse, and beyond we can see Lizard Point, and Porthleven, which looks white against the distant dark cliffs. Looking west we can see the headland of Logan Rock.

Now descend along the coast path to St Loy's Cove.

The last part of this path passes through an old woodland of oak and sycamore, which has been stunted by the sea winds. The beach is made up of granite boulders which have been formed in a way identical to that described at Cot Valley on the Botallack walk (page 60). St Loy's Cove is reputed to be the warmest cove in the UK, with many sub-tropical garden plants growing wild. 2 hrs 20 mins

Continue across the boulder-strewn beach along the coast path. Cross the small granite bridge over a stream; climb the hill, passing over a small track near St Dellan; up the hill,

Take a short detour up the valley of St Loy to enjoy bluebells in late April and early May

climb over a stile, and turn immediately right to climb over a second stile; shortly cross back over the stream using stepping stones, then turn left alongside the stream. Where the path opens out into a wider woodland, look for the end of a lane on the right; head up this lane.

Head up this lane, but first you may wish to explore the wooded valley. The wood is attractive in spring, with snowdrops in February, daffodils in March, and bluebells in late April/early May.

Continue along this minor road, passing by the wooded hamlet of Boskenna. After leaving the trees behind, the road bends right and then left; on the left-hand bend near a bungalow, go straight on through a gate on to a footpath. After passing through the gate, head towards the right, through the fence, and make for the far right-hand corner of the field. This is the lay-by at Boskenna Cross. 3 hrs

3 Sancreed to St Buryan

Beauty	***
Wildlife	**
Historical interest	*****
General interest	****
Distance	12 km (7½ miles)
Time	3½ hours
Walking conditions	Good, but some wet/muddy areas underfoot
Timing	Any season, preferably after a dry spell
Start and end point	Sancreed Beacon
Get to to start point	From A30, heading west from Penzance, take the right turning in Drift. Head for Sancreed, and in the village turn left up the hill and park after about 200 yards, on the right in a large lay-by

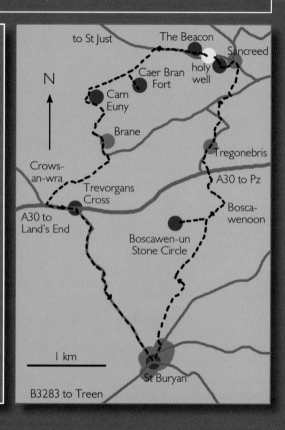

A view from Sancreed Beacon towards Mounts Bay

This is the only fully inland walk in this book, and I chose it to connect some of the most wonderful but lesser-known historical sites in the district. All of the ancient sites described here are free to enter, and it is often possible to enjoy them without crowds of people, making them spiritually more satisfying than some of the better-known examples. For reasons of practicality, the walk includes a 1½ mile stretch along a minor road; and though I have tried to avoid road-walking in this book, I think you will agree that the highlights of this walk make it worthwhile.

Caer Bran Hill Fort (above), and Holy Well near Carn Euny (right)

At the top end of the lay-by is a kissing gate leading on to the Beacon. Head to the top of the hill.

Here there are the ruins of tumuli, or burial cairns, and a great view of the surrounding area. Particularly, look south to the church tower of St Buryan: it seems a long way away, but this is on the walk! The heathland is rich in colour in the summer, with western gorse, heather and bell heather dominating.

Keep left and head down the hill back to the road. Turn right on the road, away from the lay-by. Shortly a bridleway crosses the road; turn left up this track. Where the hill levels out, you will see a path on the right and a track on the left. Turn left and walk to the top of the hill.

Here is the hill fort known as Caer Bran. The vegetation on the hill fort has been cleared to reveal its true, impressive size of approximately 70 m diameter. This is an Iron Age site, with some evidence of Bronze Age occupation. There are great views from here, and just to the right of Chapel Carn Brea it is possible to see the Isles of Scilly.

Head back down to the track and turn left; shortly the track turns left, but go straight ahead

The Iron Age settlement of Carn Euny (above), and Carn Euny fogou (left)

Carn Euny is a well-preserved courtyard house settlement. It may have been used since Neolithic times, but what we see today dates back to a period between the Iron Age and the late Roman times. Carn Euny has a wonderful 12.5 m-long fogou, which you can walk into. (A fogou is an underground tunnel; its original purpose remains a mystery.)

Exit Carn Euny through the gate at the lower end of the site, and keep right along the path which leads to a house and a lane. Follow the lane to the hamlet of Brane, and continue between the houses. Where the road bends sharply left, a track leads straight on; take this track and follow it right through a gate and between two hedges. This footpath becomes quite small where it enters a hedge beside a gate, and from here it can be quite wet under-

down a path between two hedges. Where this path meets a track at a T-junction, turn left. At the first left-hand bend there is another possible detour on the path leading off to the right, which goes a short distance to the holy well of St Euny. Continue along the main track to the left, and soon you will come across a left turn signed to Carn Euny. 45 mins

Trevorgans Cross (above), and St Buryan Church (right)

foot. Soon the path passes a caravan site on the left and comes to a track. Go straight on here (half right), and pass through the farm-yard of Cardinney, and then along the right-hand edge of two fields until you reach the A30. 1 hr 10 mins

On the A30, turn left and walk about 180 m. Here there is a right turning on a minor road to St Buryan. At the junction lies Trevorgans Cross with its incised figure. Turn right and walk along the minor road to St Buryan. 1 hr 40 mins

St Buryan provides the opportunity for lunch in the St Buryan Inn, or from the local shop. From here you will see the full height of the church tower, some 28 m high. There has been a church at this spot since about AD 930. It is said that King Athelstan stopped here, at St Buriana's chapel, during his con-quest of Cornwall, on his way to Scilly. The church tower we see today was built in 1501 using granite from Lamorna – the same stone as was used to build the Old London Bridge. Much of the surrounding church was added during the fifteenth and sixteenth centuries.

The bells in the tower include some of the heaviest in the world; the treble bell is the

Boscawen-un Stone Circle

fourth heaviest of its kind in the world; the tenor is the heaviest such bell of any six-bell peal in the world. The oldest of the bells was cast in 1638.

On the main road, turn left, and just before leaving the village take a footpath to the left between houses. In the field, head half right to the stile beside a telegraph pole. In the next field, the path crosses over a hedge to the left *and then follows along the right-hand side of the field. Cross a stile into a large field and follow the right-hand side of this field. Avoid turning right out of this field on either of two tracks; instead, follow the furthest edge of the field where it bends round to the left. About 200 m along this edge there is a small footpath over a stile to the right. This path leads down a hill into a wooded valley, over a stile and up the other*

Sancreed Church

side; bear right where there is a small parting of paths. Go over the wooden stile and up the track towards the gate. Through the gate and head straight across the middle of the open field (the left of two signed paths). Aim for the small ruined barn to the left of the house. By the gate there is a well-concealed stile. Carry straight ahead, keeping the barn on your right, and walk up the right-hand side of this field. Soon you will come to another stile which leads on to a track. Turn left on this track, and after about 400 m you will come to Boscawen-un Stone Circle. 2 hrs 30 mins

This stone circle is one of the best in Cornwall, and is situated in a romantic setting within a field enclosure. It has 19 stones, of which one is quartz, and a central standing stone that leans towards the sunrise on midsummer's day.

Return along the track, going past the stile you have just come over, all the way through the farmstead of Boscawenoon to the A30. Cross the A30 on to a footpath through two fields, and on to a minor road; turn right here. This road leads through Tregonebris; after this hamlet, where the road bends right, head straight on through a gateway on to a footpath. This path passes through a hedge, and then turns right to follow the right-hand side of the field down to the valley bottom. Continue over a stile on to the minor road, and turn left. Immediately turn right on to a footpath, and over a stile into a field. Follow the right-hand side of this field; back on to the road again, and turn right. Shortly, turn left on to a footpath just before the gate to Chiverton Farm; this footpath crosses a small field and turns right through a gateway. From here, follow the path to the left of the farm buildings. Follow the line of the telegraph poles across the open field, and this brings you to the hamlet of Sancreed.

The churchyard here contains five ancient crosses. The church is primarily thirteenth to fifteenth century in date; inside there are many interesting features, including a carved chancel screen.

Opposite the main entrance to the churchyard is a small footpath signed to the Holy Well; follow this path to the well.

Sancreed Holy Well (left). Sancreed Holy Well, cross and ruined chapel (right)

This well was rediscovered by the vicar of Sancreed in 1879. It consists of several steps down into a deep chamber, and is one of the more impressive of its type in Cornwall. Adjacent to the well are the ruins of a chapel.

Continue on the path through the site of the well, and the small path leads back to the road adjacent to the lay-by where the walk started. 3 hrs 30 mins

4 Penberth to Gwennap Head

Beauty	*****
Wildlife	****
Historical interest	***
General interest	*****
Distance	16 km (10 miles)
Time	4 hours
Walking conditions	Rocky in places; some steep hills; one wet path; very exposed to wind and rain
Timing	Low tide good to see beach of Pedn-vounder
Start and end point	Some roadside parking in Penberth (SW 402 228), where route starts; or pay-and-display car-park at Porthcurno (SW 384 226) or Porthgwarra (SW 371 218); or St Levan (SW 381 222), honesty box; or Treen (SW 394 230), pay-and-display. Start walk from any of these
Get to to start point	A30 west from Penzance, turn left at Catchall, signed St Buryan and Minack Theatre. After steep hill down and hair-pin, take next left to Penberth. Or stay on road, take next left for Treen; next left for Porthcurno and St Levan; next left for Porthgwarra (narrow, long road, passing places)

The fishing cove of Penberth

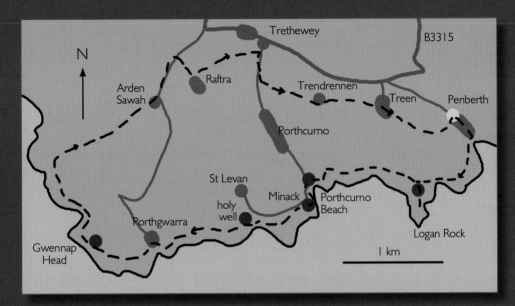

If I had to choose the most beautiful stretch of coastline in Cornwall, I think this would be it. The beaches and headlands between Penberth and Gwennap Head are astonishing. The only problem with this walk is that there are so many distractions along the way that you probably won't make it all the way before finding that it's time to return to the car. I have made this into a circular walk by including an inland return route. The advantage of this is that it is much quicker than the coastal path and takes in the pub at Treen.

The view of Pednvounder Beach from Treryn Dinas

From the roadside parking in Penberth, continue along the road on foot to the cove and take the coastal path to the right (west). Note that dogs are not allowed around the fishing cove, so if you have a dog you have to take an alternative route: from the road take the track to the right where there is a sign saying 'no parking, turning circle'; at the end of this track, turn left and this footpath leads to the cove and the coast path.

The footpath rises steeply up steps to Cribba Head and Treen Cliffs. From here enjoy the first view of Logan Rock and Treryn Dinas before continuing along the coast path to have a closer look. 30 mins

On the headland of Treryn Dinas is an Iron Age cliff castle. Turning left off the coastal path, we immediately step through the remains of a massive earth bank which was once the main defence of this fortress. On the headland is situated the famous Logan Rock. This huge granite boulder was at one time finely balanced here, and could be gently rocked with very little pressure. Understandably, this was

Logan Rock and Treryn Dinas from Porthcurno

a tourist attraction and held in great esteem by the locals, until a certain Lt. Goldsmith of the Royal Navy and his crew from HMS *Nimble* thought it would be a good idea to push the rock off the cliff, causing it to crash down to the sea below.

This horrific act of vandalism caused huge offence. It was decided that Lt Goldsmith, with the help of the Navy, should replace the rock. Replace it they did, but it took 60 men around seven months, and cost over £130 to achieve this. Since Logan Rock was replaced in 1824, no one has dared to try to loosen its hold on the cliff top!

Before leaving the headland, take time to enjoy the views to the west. This is one of the most striking views in Cornwall: the turquoise water, bright sandy beaches and rugged cliffs are stunning.

Leaving the headland, continue along the coast path. Soon there is a choice of paths; turn left for the more rugged route with better views and access to a small path down to Pednvounder (used as a naturist beach). Going down to the beach will surely mean you don't complete this walk; it is so beautiful you will want to spend time there: the choice is yours!

Along this stretch of path is a commemorative plaque on a large, white pyramidal structure. This marks the point at which one of the telegraph cables from France came ashore.

Shortly there is another choice of path. Turning left along the coast path is quicker, leading down to Porthcurno beach; turning right is an easier path, but this leads to Porthcurno with its car-park and museum. 1 hr

Porthcurno was the point at which, in 1870, telegraph cables connecting Britain to India came to land. From here the network expanded, and the telegraph company based its operations at Porthcurno, so the world's largest cable station developed here in this small Cornish cove. The significance of the station to world communications came to the fore in wartime, and in both World Wars soldiers were stationed here as protection.

During the Second World War, local miners excavated tunnels into the cliff, and a telegraph station was constructed underground, safe from enemy bombs. Today this is part of the Porthcurno Telegraph Museum, which provides a fascinating insight into the history of communications before computers and satellites linked us all together.

Eventually, all the cables came ashore on the beach, and the insignificant-looking hut that brought them all together can still be seen there.

There are plenty of things to see and do in Porthcurno: a beautiful beach, some shops selling food, and the Telegraph Museum.

Steps leading up from the beach take us quickly to a great height, from where we can look back over Porthcurno. Eventually, the steps take us to the Minack Theatre.

The theatre nestles into the cliff top so that the audience, seated on a rocky slope, faces a stage backed by the open sea. It was built in the 1930s by Rowena Cade, starting out as a project in her back garden but developing and growing into a renowned auditorium. What wonderful vision she possessed: this amphitheatre is an amazing place to watch performances, and must be an inspirational place to perform. Today the theatre runs a season of performances from May to September, while a visitor centre charts the history of the place, offering us another distraction along our route!

The coast path has many more tremendous views in store as we continue west.

From the next summit, we look down into Porth Chapel. Descending, we find yet another beach which could be visited by tak-

Porth Chapel beach, and St Levan's holy well

ing a detour off the coast path, but a short distance further is the ancient holy well of St Levan. Up some more steps and along a rocky stretch of coast path, and we soon approach Porthgwarra. 2 hrs

Porthgwarra is a small fishing cove which, like Penberth, is still in use today. A tunnel cut through solid rock to the cobbled slipway enables fishermen to take their boats down to the water. A small shop, some conveniences and a car-park are all the public services here. Today, this is a popular spot with birdwatch-ers, as the valley attracts many migrant birds in spring and autumn. Further along the coast path, we come to Gwennap Head where

Clockwise from left: Porthgwarra; Gwennap Head lookout, and The Three Chimneys

a National Coastwatch institute lookout is manned by volunteers. On this headland are a wonderful array of granite boulders carved by wind, salt spray and rain. On the ground is a form of heathland known as waved heath, because of its wave-like appearance.

Continue past the lookout; down the next valley and up the other side, staying on the path closest to the cliff top. Shortly you will come to a kissing gate passing through a wall; go through this and then bear right. Continue in this direction until it is possible to turn right on a footpath heading for the white house with three chimneys, on the horizon. 2 hrs 40 mins

Continue to and around Arden Sawah Farm, and turn left on the minor road. Take the first

A view of Chapel Carn Brea from the footpath near Treen

turning right on to a lane leading to Raftra. Immediately after Glossop Farm, turn left on to a footpath. One length of this path can be flooded after wet weather. This path meets another minor road at Trethewey; turn right here. After about 200 m, the road bends right; take the footpath to the left leading from a lay-by.

This path leads to Trendrennen Farm. Skirt the right-hand side of the buildings and turn left immediately after. A footpath leads off to the right from here across a field, and this leads to the village of Treen.

The view from this footpath across to the hills of West Penwith is a highlight of the walk, and once in Treen there is the option of visiting the Logan Rock pub, or taking refreshments at a café. 3 hrs 40 mins

To return to Penberth, take the footpath along the side of the car-park in Treen. This leads across a couple of fields and down into the valley through woodland. Once at the bottom of the hill, turn left then right to return to the car. 4 hrs

5 Land's End, Sennen and Nanjizal

Beauty	*****
Wildlife	****
Historical interest	***
General interest	*****
Distance	10 km (6¼ miles)
Time	2¾ hours
Walking conditions	Rocky in places; some steep hills; one narrow kissing gate; very exposed to wind and rain
Timing	Low tide good for seeing beach at Nanjizal
Start and end point	Land's End car-park (SW 345 250), charge for parking
Get to to start point	Follow A30 west from Penzance until it ends

The beach at Nanjizal

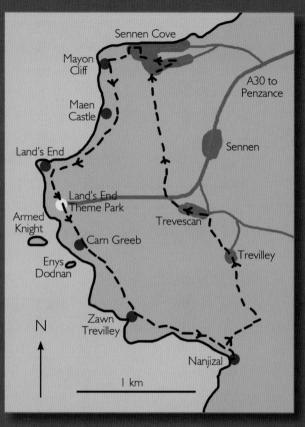

This walk takes in some of the most dramatic coastal scenery in the county, as well as the delightful Sennen Cove and the hidden gem of Nanjizal Beach. By starting at Land's End in the morning (between 10 and 10.30 a.m.), it is possible to stop for lunch at Sennen Cove, or, if you start a little later, try a packed lunch on the beach at Nanjizal. There is plenty of car-parking at Land's End, but you could catch a bus from Penzance to this starting point.

Land's End with the sea stack of Armed Knight and arch of Enys Dodnan

From the car-park, head south along the coast path. This route is a simple one, just following the coast path until you reach Nanjizal Bay.

The headland around Land's End is exceptional for flowers in summer; these include heather, bell heather, cross-leaved heath and western gorse. Also here is a colony of adders, so watch out for these creatures basking in summer – usually there is less danger when there are plenty of people using the paths! There are always a lot of jackdaws around the Land's End complex, but look out for an occasional chough and ravens.

After a short distance, the coastal path passes through Greeb Animal Farm, an attraction mostly for the kids, but there are few open farms that have such a tremendous outlook. The headland here is called Carn Greeb

– literally 'rocky ridge' – and on it have been found a flint spear and arrowheads, evidence of a Mesolithic camp here (8000–3000 BC).

The view from Pordenack Point, back towards Land's End and out to sea, is exceptional. The rocks and arch of Enys Dodnan lie closest to the land, while the Armed Knight is slightly further away (seabirds nesting on these rocks include razorbill, guillemot, fulmar and shag); further still you may be able to make out the waves breaking on the rocky islet of Kettle's Bottom, and then Longships Lighthouse is an obvious feature sitting on a long ridge of rocks standing proud of the sea. Even more distant, it might be possible to see the outline of the Isles of Scilly: to the north is Round Island Lighthouse, to the south is the island of St Mary's; between them lies St Martin's.

Continuing along the coast path, there is a deep gulley known as Zawn Trevilley. From the top of this zawn (a word derived from the Cornish *sawan* – a deep chasm in a coastal cliff), the eye is taken to another distant lighthouse – Wolf Rock Lighthouse.

Climbing up to Trevilley Cliff, we get our first view of the bay of Nanjizal (meaning 'low valley'). On the inward side of the path, look for the ancient field systems characterized by old stone walls separating very small fields.

A cave at Nanjizal

Also along this stretch, there are at least three caves into the granite which have been worked by miners looking for tin and copper. Above the caves on the granite, look at the wonderful bearded shapes of the Ramalina lichens. Common flowers along this stretch include the wild carrot (notice its white, domed-shaped heads in summer) and rock samphire (a plant with succulent leaves and yellowish-green head of flowers).

Before reaching the beach, there is a footpath sign to the left. This is the path we will take, but it is worth walking down to the beach and then returning to this point.

Walking down to the beach takes us past an old waterwheel pit. The wall of the pit is still in remarkably good condition; there would have been a leat bringing water to the left-hand side of this wheel pit. This waterwheel was once used to power the mining industry. Down on the beach there is a wonderful 'arch' in the headland to the south; incredibly tall and narrow, it was created by the action of the ocean forcing a gap through a line of weakness in the granite. Also at the back of this beach is another extraordinary feature – a very deep cave which is only accessible at low tide. This is a great beach to spend some time on, and because people have to walk here, it tends to be quieter than most! 1 hr

Go back up to the footpath sign, and head inland. This stretch of the path is steep and rocky with loose stones, so be careful.

As the hill levels out, the path is surrounded by gorse. Look out for two birds in particular – stonechats (all year) and whitethroats (May–August). Along this path the distant view is of the church at St Buryan. There is a footpath which leads down to the right, and it might be worth a short exploration to the valley bottom if you are interested in bird-watching, because this spot is good for rare migrants in autumn.

Continue along the footpath. It bends to the left, through a large kissing gate and across the middle of an arable field.

The fields here are usually sown with an arable crop, among which it is possible to find many flowers, known as 'arable weeds'. In particular, look for field pansy, corn marigold, poppy, green field speedwell, cornflower, scentless mayweed and field madder. Birds here include the skylark and meadow pipit. As the path heads upwards slightly, look inland to the beacon of Chapel Carn Brea.

This path leads easily to the hamlet of Trevilley. The footpath goes left over a stile just after a left turning from the track, about 20 m past Trevilley Farmhouse. Once past the farm buildings and into the field, keep to the right alongside the wall. This soon brings you to the houses of Trevescan, where you turn left on the B3315. 1 hr 15 mins

From here there is a quick route back to the car-park along the A30 to Land's End, but for the full walk continue along this road for about 200 m until it reaches the A30. Cross this

The footpath crosses arable fields near Trevilley

main road into the track opposite. Where the track bends to the left, keep straight on into the small footpath. This leads into a field where you should head upwards across the centre of the field (don't be tempted to follow the left-hand edge of the field). Make for a small metal kissing gate through the hedge – this is a bit of a tight one! Now head for the old Sennen Coastguard Station buildings (built in 1812) which look out to sea from the high point above Mayon Cliff.

There are many ways down to Sennen Cove, but a pleasant route is to turn right on the small road, and then left at the first footpath sign. This is a gentle descent, giving lovely views over Whitesand Bay.

Beside this path is a small leat in which you can see the tiny flowers of pink purslane. Once in Sennen, there is plenty to occupy some time. It is a great place for lunch; to sit on the beach, or look at the galleries. One gallery with plenty of character is the Round

Sennen Cove seen from Mayon Cliff (left). Waves break over the jetty at Sennen Cove (right)

House at the western end of the cove. This circular building dates back to 1876. The lower part housed a capstan to pull boats up the beach; the upper part was used for jobs such as net-mending. 2 hrs 15 mins

After time in Sennen, head west and back on to the coast path towards Land's End.

Around the coast path in Sennen there is a lot of montbretia, an invasive garden plant with orange flowers and tall, iris-like leaves. This is a popular section of the coast path, leading up a steep hill to an old lookout on Mayon Cliff. The lookout was built in 1912, and used until the 1940s. It is now owned by the National Trust, and is an information point for visitors, with powerful binoculars and telescopes to watch creatures at sea.

Heather and western gorse in flower near Land's End

Flowers along this stretch of the coastline include spring squill in April/May, and the heath spotted orchid in June. Look out for kestrels hovering or perching on rocks, and maybe a fly-past by a peregrine falcon.

After the descent from Mayon Cliff, the next cove is where the RMS *Mulheim* was wrecked in 2003. It may still be possible to see some of its hull on the rocks. Just beyond this inaccessible cove, known as Castle Zawn, is a small headland on which are the remains of a cliff castle dating back to the fifth

century BC. The walls of this castle, along with a substantial ditch, are still visible today.

From here it isn't far back to the Land's End area. This complex is very popular with tourists, and is a good place to keep children entertained. It is the most westerly point in England, and commands fantastic views. If you are interested in wildlife, then don't miss the RSPB 'discovery centre' situated beneath the hotel. Here there is information about what birds have been seen, and there may be reports of whales and dolphins as well.

6 Nanjulian to Sennen

Beauty	*****
Wildlife	****
Historical interest	***
General interest	***
Distance	10 km (6½ miles)
Time	3 hours
Walking conditions	Good, but a couple of likely damp spots and one difficult rocky section
Timing	At its best in summer for flowers. Walking the first stretch at low tide allows more time on the beach, but is not essential
Start and end point	Nanjulian (SW 362 293)
Get to to start point	From St Just take B3306 towards the airfield. After passing through Kelynack valley, take the next right – a minor road just by a house and immediately before the airfield. Follow this road to the end and park in a small lay-by on the right
Dogs	Not allowed on beach near Sennen Easter to end September, but this doesn't stop you following this walk

Nanjulian Cliff, heathland in flower

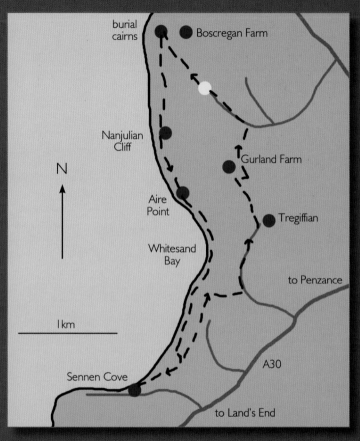

burial
cairns

Boscregan Farm

Nanjulian
Cliff

N

Gurland Farm

Aire
Point

Tregiffian

Whitesand
Bay

to Penzance

1 km

A30

Sennen Cove

to Land's End

This is a walk along a beautiful stretch of coastline with views out to the Scillies. A combination of rocky coastline and a wonderful white beach make it a delight. During summer, there is a wealth of wildflowers to be seen in the fields and on the coast. Lunch stop is in the attractive Sennen Cove.

A cairn with a granite boulder (left). The view to Sennen from Nanjulian (above)

There is a small path to the left, just past the converted mill house, and this is the shortest route to the coast path, but continue a few more metres to find a gate. Pass through this gate and carefully step through the wet patch here into the open field. Head for the highest point, straight ahead. (Please note that there are sometimes some longhorn cattle in this field; if you are afraid of cows, then take the earlier small path down to the coast and turn left on the coast path to continue the walk.)

From the lay-by, continue along the minor road past Nanjulian Farm and Nanjulian Mill (which is no longer in use).

As you walk down through this valley, keep an eye out for bird life. This is a particularly good area for migrant birds in spring and autumn (May, September and October are the best months).

On this hill there are at least three burial cairns. One contains a huge granite boulder, which was integral to its formation. It is thought that granite must have been highly valued by the people who made the cairn, probably in the early Bronze Age.

The view to Cape Cornwall from Nanjulian

To the north, along the coast, we see the famous headland of Cape Cornwall, and out to sea from there is the rocky twin island known as The Brisons. To the south, we can already see the lunchtime destination of this walk, at Sennen Cove. Beyond Sennen is the complex of buildings at Land's End, and just out to sea from there you will spot the Longships Lighthouse standing tall on a dangerous reef. Longships was first established in 1795, and now stands 35 m tall. Look a little further out, and on a clear day it is possible to see the Isles of Scilly.

Immediately inland is Boscregan Farm, a National Trust property whose fields come alive with a mass of arable flowers in June and July. At Boscregan there is one flower – purple viper's bugloss – which is found at no

Boscregan Farm with purple viper's bugloss

It is said that Charles II sheltered at Nanjulian when he was escaping from the Roundheads to the Scillies. Since his time, the valley has been used intensively for mining, and we can see the remains of mine and mill buildings here. The small river was obviously an important driving force for this industry. Be careful not to fall into the wheel pit of one of the old mills if you venture up the valley!

Look out for birds of prey in this area; there are usually kestrels and buzzards, but there may also be sparrowhawks and peregrines. It is not unusual to spot a pair of choughs feeding on the short turf near the coast here.

Continue along the coast path, climbing the steps out of the valley. From here, the going is quite easy for a while as you pass along the side of Nanjulian Cliff.

The vegetation here is typical of coastal heath – a mix of heather, bell heather and western gorse, all of which flower from July to September, so you may see a blaze of colour. Keep an eye out to sea as you can often watch seabirds passing by. This passage is at its greatest in August and September, when many shearwaters and skuas are spotted, but at any time of year we might see gannets, fulmars, auks and Manx shearwaters. I hr

Rounding the headland of Aire Point is the most difficult part of this walk. There is a bit

other site in Cornwall. It is a bold, dark purplish-blue flower, which grows in profusion, its expanse broken only by the statuesque, shapely nodding heads of barley and, in places, swathes of vivid yellow corn marigolds.

The land here is managed specifically for the arable flowers, and many more unusual species hide beneath this colourful canopy. It is acceptable for visitors to walk along the edges of these fields, and there is a convenient gateway not far from here, so have a closer look if you like, before moving on.

Head south on the coast path towards Sennen; immediately you will pass an old mine shaft around which has been constructed a wall for our safety. Shortly you will descend into the valley of Nanjulian. This is where the path from Nanjulian Mill meets the coast path.

of a clamber up rocks at first, then a steep descent soon after, but my father did it when he was 81, so I have every confidence in you!

The granite here is very interesting as it shows a range of weathering effects. Wind, rain and salt spray find weaknesses in the granite and create wonderful sculptures in this hard rock. On the surface of some boulders, you may see a layer of granite lifting like a layer of skin; this is known appropriately as onion-skin weathering. Look closely at the

Whitesand Bay (top) and Gwynver Beach (above)

Pill box and chalet above Whitesand Bay

granite and you will see that the largest crystals – those of the feldspars – often lie parallel to each other; this is because the feldspar was the first crystal to form as the molten rock cooled, and the hardened crystals continued to flow until the surrounding rock solidified.

From here, we are rewarded with a magnificent view across Whitesand Bay towards Sennen. This beach is split in two by a rocky headland; the first section is known as Gwynver Beach. If it is low tide, it will be possible to walk along the beach all the way to Sennen, with maybe a little bit of paddling around the rocks; if not, then continue along the coast path, taking care to follow all the minor diversions recently made to keep walkers safe from the crumbling edges of the cliffs.

Once the coast path descends back down to the second beach, I recommend making the final stretch on the beach into Sennen, because the alternative coast path route is slightly longer. Dog-walkers will have no choice but to follow the coast path during the daytime from Easter to September as dogs are banned from this part of the beach at this time. I hr 45 mins

The route into Sennen arrives in the main car-park, where there are facilities and places to eat. You may wish to explore Sennen Cove before returning on the suggested inland route.

To return, take the coast path back in the direction from which you came, from the corner of the car-park near the café. This path leads through the dunes and between the houses of Escalls Green. Follow the coast path beyond the houses until you are about 45 m short of the pill box and chalet overlooking the beach. Here there is a footpath to the right up the hill.

This footpath makes a gentle ascent to the top of the cliffs, with great views over the surrounding coast. It can be a bit damp underfoot, but you can usually avoid getting too muddy.

At the top of the hill, continue at roughly the same level; there are a variety of small paths. At the top of Escalls Cliff there is only one path, which leads inland. You soon fork left, and left again on a path between two walls, which leads to a thatched cottage called Poldown. Continue on the track past this cottage until you meet a minor road, and here turn left again.

This minor road leads to a small car-park. Go straight on past here. Soon a footpath sign to Nanquidno indicates that you are on the correct track. Go straight on. The road deteriorates into a track, and zig-zags a little through farmland. On the final, right-hand bend, be-

Escalls Green on the coast path near Sennen

fore a complex of houses at Tregiffian, is a track heading off left (effectively straight on) following a line of telegraph poles. Take this track.

This heads to Gurland Farm. Two fields before the farm, take the footpath to the right along the edge of a field. It soon cuts left through the hedge and across two fields, before coming to a gate. Through the gate, turn right on the track, which leads down and up to the road where you parked. Turn left on this small road, and you will soon be back at the lay-by. 3 hrs

7 Botallack to Cot Valley

Beauty	*****
Wildlife	****
Historical interest	*****
General interest	****
Distance	11 km (7 miles)
Time	3¾ hours
Walking conditions	Very good, though exposed to westerly wind
Timing	Mostly historical interest, so any time of year
Start and end point	Botallack Count House (SW 365 332)
Get to to start point	From St Just head north on B3306. On entering Botallack turn left, passing the Queen's Arms on the right. Where the road bends right, turn left on to a track. Follow this road to the Count House

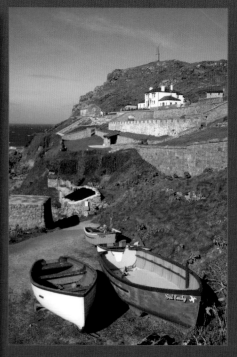

Cape Cornwall from Priest's Cove

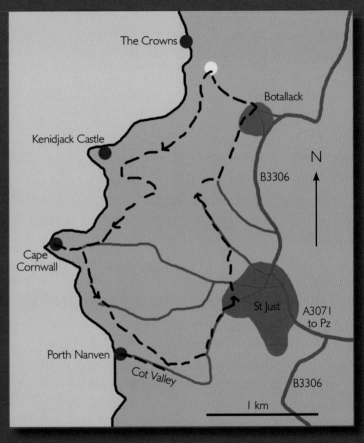

The Crowns

Botallack

Kenidjack Castle

N

B3306

Cape
Cornwall

St Just

A3071
to Pz

Porth Nanven

Cot Valley

B3306

1 km

This is a very interesting walk, because not only does it lead us through some of the World Heritage site for mining, but it also links three of the county's most iconic places:

The Crowns engine houses, Cape Cornwall and Cot Valley. Not a fast walk, as there is lots to see and a few detours to add in.

The calciner (above) and The Crowns engine houses (left) at Botallack

There is plenty to explore immediately around the car-park. First, have a look in the Count House, where an information centre details some of the historical and wildlife interest of the area. Just over the road from the Count House is the Brunton calciner, a labyrinth of stone walls and arches built in 1908. It was a flue in which arsenic-laden fumes were carried to the chimney. Arsenic was a

The view into Kenidjack Valley from the coast path (left). Kenidjack Valley with the mill pond (right)

by-product of the tin process, and because it had a value, this flue was created to allow the arsenic to condense on to its inner surface, from where it was scraped off manually.

A few metres to the north of here you may see the remains of many other tin-mining buildings. Here also are some circular buddles, which were used as part of the process for separating tin from waste.

Looking down to the sea from here you will notice The Crowns engine houses at the base of the cliffs. This is one of the most famous Cornish mining landmarks. From here, miners worked shafts and adits more than half a mile out under the sea. Mining operations at The Crowns eventually ceased at the beginning of the twentieth century. 30 mins

Take the coast path to the south, and soon, on the left, you will pass the engine house of West Wheal Owles.

Here, in 1893, there was a dramatic and catastrophic accident when miners blasted a way through into a nearby flooded mine. The force of inrushing water left the 19 men and one boy with no chance; their bodies are still underground. To the right is Wheal Edward.

On the headland of Kenidjack Castle there are a couple of interesting features. The two linear walls and earth mounds are the remains of late nineteenth-century rifle ranges; the trench in front of one is where targets were raised from. On the cliff to the seaward side of the rifle ranges are the remains of an

Cape Cornwall seen from Kenidjack Valley

Iron Age cliff castle; it is just possible to make out the ramparts as earth banks and dips.

Look out for the cocoons of oak eggar moths here during the summer. They are papery and brown, resembling soft acorns, hence the name of the moth.

The view over Kenidjack Valley has changed a lot in the last two centuries. This was once a major mining area; the linear earthworks on the opposite valley slope are the remains of leats which carried water from the top of the valley to power waterwheels in the mines at the foot of the valley, near the beach of Porthledden Cove.

Notice also the mill pond in the valley, which was used to supply water for one of these leats. It has recently been renovated by the National Trust.

Walk down the path into the valley. Here the walk route follows the coast path, so turn left and then right, following the coast path signs, but you might want to make a detour down to

Porthledden Cove to have a close look at the remains of the mines. 1 hr (add 30 mins to remaining times if you detour to Porthledden)

From here, the coast path heads up the hill, and then turns right along the top of the valley towards the headland of Cape Cornwall. The footpath leads to the small road down to the car-park for Cape Cornwall. Turn right on this road, and head for the monument on top of the headland.

It is worth climbing to the summit for the commanding views of the surrounding coastline. On top of the headland is a chimney, built to improve the draught for the boiler house of the Cape Cornwall Mine, which is now the furthest private house. The large white house was once the home of the captain of the mine. Cape Cornwall is the only cape in England, and isn't technically a cape since it isn't at the point between two oceans. Now the headland is used by volunteers of the National Coastwatch Institute. 1 hr 30 mins

Return down the hill, and turn right before the car-park on to the coast path.

The cove here is known as Priest's Cove. It is home to a small selection of fishing boats. Look around the cliffs near the fishing huts to see the succulent leaves and both pink and yellow flowers of Hottentot fig, an invasive weed now smothering our native flowers.

Continue along the coast path to the south, up the hill by the golf course, and on to a small road at the top of the hill. This is Carn Gloose. Take a short detour (approx 50 m) along this road to see Ballowall Barrow.

Carn Gloose is a beautiful headland with terrific views. Out to sea are the rocks known as The Brisons; slightly more distant is the Longships Lighthouse, and on a good day the Scillies are visible. Ballowall Barrow is a striking Bronze Age burial cairn. Its remains were concealed by waste from the mining industry until their discovery by William Borlase in the late nineteenth century. He built walls, which changed the barrow's appearance, but this remains a fascinating monument.

Head back on to the coast path, and continue southwards. The path leads down a hill along the side of Cot Valley, a somewhat similar valley to Kenidjack but with fewer obvious remains of mining.

Before you reach the road at the bottom of the valley, you will come to a junction of footpaths just before a small copse. Turn left here, and walk back up the valley side to begin the return leg of the walk; but before you do, turn right and walk down to the mouth of the valley to enjoy Porth Nanven. 2 hrs 15 mins

Cot Valley is famous among birdwatchers for being a great place for seeing rare

Cot Valley and The Brisons (top). The cliff in Porth Nanven, at the foot of Cot Valley (above)

birds, particularly in autumn. In fact, any of the valleys on the west coast of Penwith can produce interesting finds in September and October. The little cove of Porth Nanven is well known for its beautifully rounded boulders. Photographers love them because they make great foreground for landscape photos, and people have been known to steal them, though this should not be considered as they are an important part of the valley's history.

The majority of the boulders on the beach here are very smoothly worn. The story of their formation is told on an interpretive board under the cliff at the top of the beach, and this story can be seen within the cliff itself. Looking at the cliff, you will see that the rounded boulders are found at the bottom; packed on top are more angular rock fragments. The rounded boulders were worn by the sea rolling them around, taking off the sharp edges until they were perfectly smooth. During the last Ice Age, as the sea levels dropped, these stones were left high and dry. Gradually, as a result of freezing and thawing, the smooth stones were packed in with debris from the surrounding hilltops, and shards of sharper rocks slipped down the slopes on top. Then, with the end of the Ice Age, came a rise in sea levels, and the waves began cutting back into the cliffs, releasing the stones from their incarceration to roll around on the beach again.

Head back to the junction of footpaths, and up the valley side again. This section of footpath is a little tricky underfoot, and it is possible to avoid it by simply walking straight up the small road out of the valley. If you take the footpath, you will come out on to a small track on which you turn right, and then this will meet the same road at Bosorne, where you will need to turn left and walk as far as the edge of St Just.

Turn left into Pleasant Terrace. At the end of this path, turn left and immediately right on to a footpath across the school playing fields. At the end of the path, again turn left and immediately right on to another footpath. Soon you will come to a road; turn left and walk as far as Boscean. Continue on the road, which becomes a track and turns right after the farm. Here the track splits into two footpaths: take the right-hand path, down the hill.

Notice from here the small fields on the opposite side of the valley. These were used by miners to grow their own potatoes in the middle of the nineteenth century.

At the bottom of the valley, cross the river, turn right then immediately left up a steep, windy track through some ruined buildings. Keep going straight on over stiles, then right and left past a private building, once the Wheal Owles

Stream, Kenidjack Valley (top). A view back towards Botallack from the return footpath (above)

Count House, and alongside the cricket pitch. Soon this track splits. Turn right here to return to Botallack by the Queens Head pub if you want sustenance, or turn left and immediately right on to a footpath straight across a field if you want to return to the car-park by a slightly shorter route. This brings you on to a small road with houses where you will go straight on; then turn left at the road junction to go back down the track to the car-park. 3 hrs 45 mins

8 Rosemergy to Morvah including Men-an-Tol

Beauty	*****
Wildlife	***
Historical interest	*****
General interest	***
Distance	11 km (7 miles)
Time	3½ hours
Walking conditions	Rocky in places, particularly along coast path; moorland very exposed to wind
Timing	Mostly historical interest, so any time of year
Start and end point	Lay-by beside B3306, St Ives to Pendeen road, adjacent to Rosemergy engine house below Carn Galver Hill (SW 421 364)
Get to to start point	From A30, Penzance by-pass, take road to Madron. Drive to the end of this road, turn right on B3306. Park on left in about one mile

Rosemergy engine house

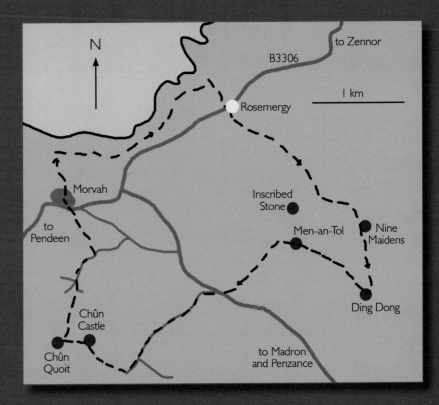

N

to Zennor

B3306

1 km

Rosemergy

Morvah

to
Pendeen

Inscribed
Stone

Men-an-Tol

Nine
Maidens

Ding Dong

Chûn
Castle

Chûn
Quoit

to Madron
and Penzance

This is a walk I have planned for maximum historical interest. It includes engine houses, stone circles, a quoit, standing stones, a Bronze Age hill-top castle, and the famous stones of Men-an-Tol. The route crosses wet moorland, which is very exposed, and returns along one of the most difficult stretches of coast path in the county, so it is not to be undertaken lightly. There is the opportunity for refreshments three-quarters of the way round at the School House Gallery and Coffee Shop in Morvah, but it is wise to check on its opening times if depending upon it (tel. no. 01736 787808).

From the lay-by, follow the main road for about 50 m to the west, turning left into the first footpath. Follow this path to the top of the hill.

Where the path reaches its highest point, there is an optional detour to the summit of Carn Galver, to the left. This is one of the most distinctive hills in this area, and its height affords lovely views of the surrounding area.

Continuing on the same footpath, you soon come to the first sight of Ding Dong engine house, which will form part of this walk. To the left is the small, craggy peak of Little Galver. The path bends a little to the right, so that it faces directly towards the distant engine house.

To the right is a standing stone. This 1.8 m-high stone, known as Men Scryfa ('stone of writing'), was erected in the Bronze Age, and has a Celtic inscription to commemorate Rialobranus, 'Royal Raven son of the glorious prince', who is thought to have died in battle here. Beyond this stone, on top of the distant hill of Carn Bean, is a beacon used to control air traffic heading to or from America.

When the footpath approaches a ruined building on the right there is a junction; turn left here, and head for the top of the nearby small hill.

On top of this hill are stone circles and cairns. The main circle is known as Nine Maidens – a bit of a misnomer since originally there were probably 22 stones in the circle. Now only six stones remain, standing to an average height of about 1.2 m. The name 'Nine Maidens' is used for a number of stone circles, and it is likely that it was used at this site by mistake, but became accepted.

After looking at the stones, continue in the same direction towards the engine house. 1 hr

Ding Dong mine is reputed to be the oldest mine in Cornwall. It is said to have been worked for over 2,000 years, though the earliest recorded workings were at the beginning of the seventeenth century. Richard Trevithick was once the engineer at this mine, and while here he developed a successful high pressure engine. Trevithick also invented the first self-propelled road locomotive – the *Puffing Devil*. There is a stunning view from the foot of this engine house. Looking in a roughly south-easterly direction, it is possible to see St Michael's Mount and Mount's Bay. To the left of this are the summits of Tregonning Hill and Godolphin Hill; to the left and slightly nearer is the peak of Castle-an-Dinas, complete with the folly of Roger's Tower.

From Ding Dong, turn right as if heading for the summit of Carn Galver. This brings us shortly to Men-an-tol.

Men-an-tol is a mystery: a unique megalithic monument of which we have no real

One of the stones of the Nine Maidens Stone Circle with the summit of Carn Galver in the background (left). Ding Dong Engine House (right)

understanding. Men-an-Tol means 'holed stone', but this is a stone between two standing stones, possibly within the remains of a stone circle.

Its size means a typical adult can pass through the hole, but only by crawling on hands and knees. To either side of this stone are standing stones about 1.2 m high, which can be viewed through the hole. Inevitably, people have tried to discover reasons for this creation. Observations of lunar movements have suggested that the position of the moon may have had an influence; other possibilities are that the holed stone was moved here from elsewhere at a later date, or perhaps it was part of a tomb.

The curious stones of Men-an-Tol

The site has become the subject of many local superstitions, most notably that the stone has healing powers. Children could be cured of tuberculosis or rickets if passed naked through the stone three times. Adults could be cured of spinal problems if they passed three times through the hole against the sun. There are other superstitions to do with fertility and rheumatism, to name two.

Continue along the same footpath until you come to a stile. Go over this, and then turn left on to the main track. This leads down to the road between Madron and the coast road. Turn right and immediately left, signed to Chûn Castle. This is a very quiet road, leading only to Trehyllys Farm. Pass through the farm and bear right, heading for the white stone that marks the route to the top of the hill on which Chûn Castle is situated. 1 hr 45 mins

Chûn Castle is at the summit of the hill, just to the right of the path. It is about 85 m in diameter. The large stone gateposts marking its entrance still stand, but its walls are no more than circular piles of rubble, much of

The view from Chûn Castle

which, it is said, was removed to build the streets of Penzance. The castle was originally built in the second or third century BC, and was built upon again in the sixth century AD.

This area is Chûn Downs, a Cornwall Wildlife Trust nature reserve. In summer there is good colour with heather, bell heather and cross-leaved heath; in winter look out for occasional birds of prey, including possible hen harrier, merlin and short-eared owl.

Turning left to face Pendeen church, you see the nearby Chûn Quoit, to which we will walk.

A quoit – known in other parts of the country as a cromlech or dolmen – is a huge slab of stone lying flat like a table top, supported by several upright stones. This arrangement produces a large stone box or chamber, once used to hold remains of the dead. It is likely that a quoit would have been the centrepiece of ritual and ceremony, with the larger examples acting as a symbol of power among the Neolithic people who built them. Originally, much of the structure of a quoit would have been covered by a mound of soil and stones,

Chûn Quoit

with perhaps just the flat capstone and maybe an entrance exposed. Chûn Quoit is one of the best preserved of all Cornish quoits; it has an eight-tonne capstone sitting robustly on its original uprights, and though there has been some collapse, it is still possible to see the intended structure.

Now turn back right, as if heading for the distant shape of Morvah Church. This footpath is well signed, and leads down to a track. At the first small junction turn left, and then at the crossroads of tracks, turn right. This track becomes a road, and before reaching Carne Farm there is a footpath on the left. This path is fairly easy to follow as it crosses a few small fields and then emerges on the B3306 coast road. Turn left, and then immediately right into the hamlet of Morvah. 2 hrs 15 mins

In Morvah, pause to look at the church. Originally dedicated to St Morwetha, in 1409, it was soon dedicated to St Bridget of Sweden, who founded the Order of the Bridgentines in 1373. Legend suggests a local man, Jack the Giant Killer, trapped Cormoran, the Cornish giant from St Michael's Mount, by digging a huge pit and disguising it

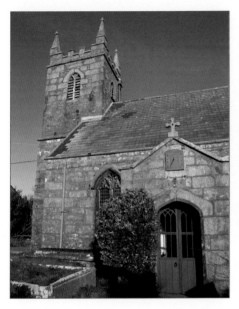

Morvah Church (left). A view along the cliffs between Morvah and Bosigran (right)

with sticks. He lured him into the hole using his horn; killed him, and claimed a reward. The large stone in Morvah churchyard is said to be the one that caps the pit.

The route from here follows the footpath beside the church signed to the coast path. Walk as far as the coast path and turn right.

This is a beautiful stretch of coast, with wonderful views to Gurnard's Head. It is popular with rock climbers, indicating that it is very rocky, so take great care. Look out for the beautiful heath-spotted orchid in June.

Eventually, you will come to a deep valley with ruined mine buildings at the bottom. Turn right at the foot of the valley, and this path will lead directly back to Rosemergy Engine House and lay-by. In the wooded area, keep right rather than taking the small footpath to the left, which leads to the Climber's House nearby. 3 hrs 30 mins

9 Trevalgan to St Ives

Beauty	*****
Wildlife	****
Historical interest	**
General interest	****
Distance	14 km (8¾ miles)
Time	3¾ hours
Walking conditions	Rocky in places; some steep hills; many granite stiles to climb over; very exposed to rain and north wind
Timing	A lovely walk when heathland flowers in full bloom (Aug/Sept)
Start and end point	Lay-by beside B3306, St Ives to Zennor road, at summit between Trevalgan Hill and Rosewall Hill (SW 487 394)
Get to to start point	From St Ives take B3306 towards Zennor. The lay-by is about 1½ miles from outskirts of St Ives
Warning	Strong likelihood of encountering cattle

River Cove with The Carracks in the distance

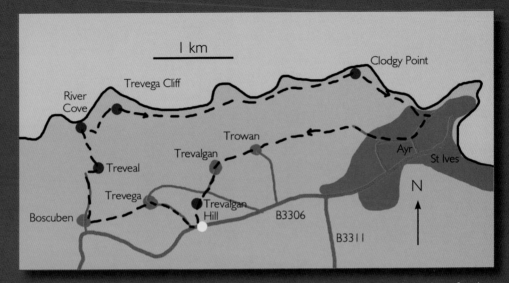

This is a walk of contrasts. Its coastal section is rough, rugged and difficult, yet impressive and irresistible. Inland, the landscape is mellow as it crosses the many small fields of Iron Age origin, but the granite moorland is never far away, and even this section of path is made challenging by the frequent granite step stiles. I have chosen the starting point and route for this walk so that it is possible to take a long break in St Ives for lunch.

A view towards Trevail Valley from near Trendrine (above). On the coast near Pen Enys Point (right)

From the lay-by, follow the main road for about 50 m to the west, and turn right on to the first minor road. Ignore the first footpath to the left, but then immediately after Trevessa Farm turn left on to a footpath.

Trevessa Farm was the birthplace of Sir John Quick, a founding member of the Commonwealth of Australia (see the plaque on the farmhouse wall). The footpath soon dips into a small valley through which the Treveal Stream flows; this is the same valley that we will pass again on the way east along the coast to St Ives. Growing in the marshy ground beside the river is the poisonous hemlock water dropwort, which has umbels of white flowers in early summer. The trees here are laden with luxuriant lichens. On the stone stiles and walls in this area, look for the unusual navelwort – a plant with many shield-like round leaves and a tall spike of greenish flowers, so typical of west Cornwall.

The route of this path is easy to follow as it passes through variously shaped fields. Keep going straight on through Trendrine Farm; turn right on the track just before Boscubben. On approaching Treveal, follow the footpath sign to the right for St Ives. This dips down a hill towards Trevail Mill. Turn left before entering the grounds of the mill.

The small hamlet of Treveal was once a thriving community owned by the Hain Estate, which operated a shipping company. Most of the people in this hamlet would have been involved in fishing or mining. Trevail Mill is now privately owned, but was once the site of two corn mills. The first records of activity here come from the sixteenth century, though it is likely that the stream was used by 'miners' before then. There is evidence that the stream was used to power the tin-mining processes in the nineteenth century.

Having turned left on to a small footpath, signed to River Cove and St Ives, the path takes in woodland, riverside, and finally open heath. This mixed habitat is good for a variety of birds, including migrants in spring and autumn. I hr

At the junction with the coast path, turn right. The signpost states 'St Ives 3½ miles', but this is one of the longer 3½ miles that I can remember walking, not because it is a drag but because it is very difficult walking in places.

The first dip in the path is to cross the Treveal Valley. Its associated cove is called River

Cattle graze the coastline

Cove. Take a small detour to look into the cove; there may be grey seals hauled out on the beach here, but if not, scan the sea and the distant rock islets called The Carracks.

Progressing along the coast path, the quality of the heathland improves up to the summit of Trevega Cliff, where there is a triangulation point. From here it is possible to see along the north coast of Cornwall as far as Trevose Head, a distance of about 33 miles, and it is only the shape of the coastline that prevents us seeing any further. This spectacular view is punctuated by many familiar Cornish landmarks, including St Agnes Beacon and Godrevy Lighthouse.

The heath comes alive in late summer with heather, bell heather and western gorse all in flower during August and early September.

Porthmeor Beach, St Ives

The area around Treveal and Trevega is owned by the National Trust; other areas owned by the Trust along this route include Pen Enys Point and Hor Point, otherwise the land is privately owned. The coast path follows a short section of the Trevalgan Farm trail, a walk established by owners of this farm for use by people staying on their campsite and in the self-catering accom- modation. Information panels on the trail include a story of the shipwreck of SS *Besse- mer City* in 1941, which was carrying tinned food. All the sailors on board the ship were saved, but unfortunately, before the cargo could be rescued, the labels were washed off the tins, leaving people who had gath- ered them to wonder what they might be having for tea that night!

The pretty town of St Ives makes a wonderful destination for this walk

Pen Enys Point is a wonderful spot for its flora. The damp ground holds royal fern, southern marsh orchids (June) and butterwort (May to July), while the drier ground has spring squill, lousewort and milkwort, and the heath has heath-spotted orchids (June). Add to this the usual mix of coastal plants, such as thrift, sea campion and wild carrot to provide colour throughout the summer.

One other noteworthy plant found here is the devilsbit scabious, which plays host to the caterpillars of the marsh fritillary, so in May and June watch out for this attractive butterfly as well.

Out to sea it is always possible to see a variety of birds at any time of year. Gannets and kittiwakes are frequent; Manx shearwaters are most often seen on summer eve-

Climbing over yet another granite stile on the return route!

nonchalant as possible, turning upside down to greet the peregrines' attacks with its own fairly deadly talons.

Following the coast path here needs no directions, just lots of stamina, and eventually you will round Clodgy Point and come into sight of St Ives and its Porthmeor Beach. I would recommend a visit to this wonderful seaside harbour town, maybe stopping for lunch, before completing the walk. 2 hrs 45 mins

To make a start on the return route, follow the road up the steep hill beside the cemetery near the Tate Gallery. Follow this road where it bends right at the top of the hill, as far as a right turning along Burthallan Lane. Head along this small lane and take a footpath to the left, signed to Zennor and Treveal.

The footpath from here to Trowan passes through a maze of small fields whose boundary hedges have remained much the same for the last two or three thousand years. Ahead of us and slightly to the left are the hills of Rosewall and Trevalgan, between which is the lay-by at the start of the walk.

The footpath leads through the hamlet of Trowan and on to Trevalgan Farm. Skirt the right-hand side of the farm, and then turn left to go up the farm lane. The fields around the farm can be quite muddy. At the end

nings. Overhead watch out for buzzards and kestrels, as well as the omnipresent ravens. On one walk in this area, I watched mesmerized as a pair of peregrines took out their anger on a raven, continually diving at it from a height; the raven's response was as

The view west from Trevalgan Hill with Treveal in the distance

of the farm lane is a footpath to the top of Trevalgan Hill.

The summit of Trevalgan Hill is a great climax to this walk, not least because from here it is possible to review the entire route and bask for a moment in the satisfaction that brings. Peter Lanyon, the famous twentieth-century artist of the St Ives School, is remembered by a plaque near the summit of this hill.

He died at a premature age in a gliding accident in 1964. From here, the end of the walk is a short distance away, and it's all downhill from here! 3 hrs 45 mins

10 Trencrom to St Ives

Beauty	*****
Wildlife	***
Historical interest	***
General interest	*****
Distance	11 km (7 miles)
Time	3 hours
Walking conditions	Rocky in places; some damp spots underfoot; some very steep hills
Timing	Any
Start and end point	Small, National Trust car-park at Trencrom Hill
Get to to start point	From A30 west of Hayle, turn towards St Ives at large roundabout. Go straight on at first mini-roundabout, then left at the next (this takes you on the back road to St Ives). After a mile there are two minor roads to the left, take the first of these signed to Cripplesease. Free car-park on right approx ½ mile
Warning	Strong likelihood of encounter-ing cattle

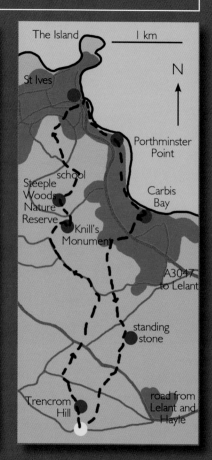

The summit and path down from Trencrom Hill on a cold winter day

This is a very interesting walk, encompassing two hills with great views over St Ives Bay and lots of attractive footpaths, with part of the route along the St Michael's Way. The highlights are Trencrom Hill and Knill's Monument, and lunch can be had in St Ives, where there is always plenty to see and do.

The ascent of Trencrom Hill with its distinctive granite boulders

From the car-park, take the path that leads directly up the hill.

On the top of Trencrom Hill, it is still possible to see the remains of a Neolithic hill fort. On the slopes here, an axe head has been found dating occupation to 3500 BC. The hill is about 170 m high, and has fantastic panoramic views: look north-east over the Hayle Estuary and St Ives Bay to Godrevy, and beyond to Trevose Head; east is the distant hill and monument of Carn Brea; look south to St Michael's Mount and the Lizard, and west to Roger's Tower on top of Castle-an-Dinas.

Continue in a straight line, heading for the large farm buildings down the north-west side of the hill. Keep heading for the buildings; cross a field, and turn left on to a small road. The road bends left just after Trencrom Cottage; turn right here on to a footpath. Follow the right-hand side of the fields for the first two fields, then cut across the third field in line with the lane on the other side of the valley. Cross the road and go up this lane. 20 mins

This leads past Trevarrack. Keep straight on until you come to a road; turn left here. Continue along this road, passing a junction to the left at Vorvas Vean. Soon after this, the road bends sharp left; turn right here on to a footpath. Shortly ahead of you and to the right is Knill's Monument on Worvas Hill. Head up to this summit. 55 mins

John Knill was born in Callington in 1733; he became the collector of customs in St Ives from 1762 to 1782, and was town Mayor in 1767. He built his own mausoleum in 1782, which is now known as Knill's Monument. It was his intention to be buried in his mausoleum, but Knill died in London and so was actually buried at Holborn.

In his will he left money for the upkeep of the mausoleum, and for celebrations to be held every five years. The parade of people includes: ten little girls; the Mayor, vicar and head of customs; a fiddler and two widows. These people and various other guests walk from the Guildhall to the monument. The money that Knill set aside also included £5 to be given to the couple that has raised the greatest family of legitimate children, each to have reached the age of ten years!

Until recently, the hill was covered in rhododendron ponticum. This has been cleared to prevent the spread of the sudden oak death fungus, and to allow the natural regeneration of heathland. Native trees have also been planted.

From the summit, head approximately north down a steep hill, and on to a small tarmac path, which soon leads to a small road. Here there is a notice board explaining the work that has been done on the hill. Cross straight over the road into Steeple Woods Nature Reserve.

This is beautiful, ancient woodland, with mature beech and oak trees.

Walk straight into the wood along the main path; over a small stream and wall, then over

Knill's Monument, constructed in 1782

a second wall before turning right. This leads on to a track down the right-hand side of the school playing fields.

Turn left on the road in front of the school, and keep straight on along a track. When you come to a road, head straight across it and up a small road ahead. Turn right on a lane

The view from Worvas Hill across St Ives Bay

opposite the car-park for Belyars Bowling Green. This leads past a house called Wetherby.

The track meanders through fields, before coming to some houses. Bear right at a fork; ignore a right turning, then turn right down the hill and over a stile by a gate. This leads down a hill, with a great view of St Ives and The Island, and soon enters the main car-park in St Ives. Follow signs down to the town. 1 hr 30 mins

You can wander through St Ives before heading off on the return leg of this walk.

From the harbour area, take the coast path out of St Ives to the east (towards Carbis Bay). After Porthminster Beach, the footpath climbs up a hill, crosses the railway line, and continues up on to a small road, known as Hain Walk.

Hain Walk was specially constructed by Sir Edward Hain, a shipping magnate born in St

Porthminster Beach (above). Baulking house (right)

Ives in 1853, for the public to enjoy views over St Ives. At the top of this climb, you will see a white building on the right. This is the Baulking House, used by 'huers' who looked for shoals of pilchards in the bay, in order to direct fishing boats towards them.

Continue along the coast path which leads down to Carbis Bay, and over the railway line again. 1 hr 55 mins

Carbis Bay Beach

After rounding the Carbis Bay Hotel, head inland under the arches of the railway viaduct. Now starts a very steep ascent! Just keep walking up the valley following the minor road and path to where it meets the main road. Cross the main road on to another small footpath, and continue straight on. This meets a road, Ros-lyn, in a housing estate. Head straight along this road, and where you come to a T-junction, turn left. Soon the road bends left; here, go straight on to a track marked as a footpath.

This track becomes a footpath and then turns into a track again; just keep going straight on. Eventually it meets a road beside a house; go straight across on to a footpath which is now part of the St Michael's Way. We will follow the St Michael's Way right back to the car-park,

A Highland Cow stands beside the path on the return to Trencrom

immediately right on to the footpath signed 'Trencrom Hill ¼ mile'. Over another stile and into a field; head to the top left-hand corner of this field; cross another stile, then the minor road, and head straight on to another section of footpath.

This is the final stretch, as this path skirts around the lower edge of Trencrom Hill and leads back to the car-park. 3 hrs

but I will give directions as the route isn't always very clear! 2 hrs 25 mins

The footpath soon leads through a caravan site; follow the way-marked signs here. Over a stile, then go across the middle of a field heading just to the left of the large barn; here there is a stile, and soon a road.

Cross the road on to a footpath and over a stile; keep to the left-hand side of the field, and soon go over a stile to the left; now follow the right-hand side of this field.

Notice the standing stone in the middle of this field.

Cross a stile on to a pleasant path between two hedges. Head down the hill past a couple of houses to the main road. Turn left, then

11 St Erth to the Hayle Estuary

Beauty	**
Wildlife	*****
Historical interest	***
General interest	****
Distance	7 km (4½ miles)
Time	1½ hours
Walking conditions	Very good, flat, only occasionally damp underfoot
Timing	Any, but fewer birds when tide fully in
Start and end point	St Erth Church car-park (SW 549 351)
Get to to start point	From A30 take turning to St Erth railway station, just west of Hayle. Continue past the station for approx ½ mile, then turn left. Immediately after crossing the narrow bridge, park on left or right

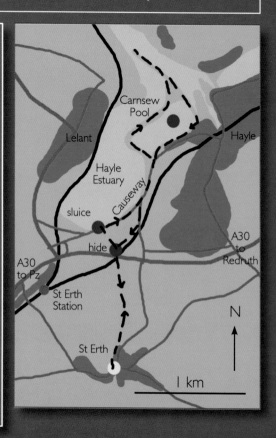

St Erth Church

This is a short walk along the River Hayle and its estuary, which is particularly good for birdwatching. There are always birds to see here: it is at its quietest for birds in June and July, though at this time there are some interesting flowers to spot. Generally, it is best not to visit the estuary at high tide as the mud flats are all covered and the birds will be more difficult to spot. Walkers should note that part of this path is along the busy road known as The Causeway. There is a footpath alongside the road, but please be very careful when crossing the road.

The River Hayle near St Erth

Start at St Erth. In the village there is a public house and a shop, so it is possible to have lunch or buy provisions here. The church in St Erth was built in 1215. The village was named after an Irish saint called St Erc. St Erth was once the main crossing point of the River Hayle, until The Causeway was built alongside the main estuary between the two World Wars.

You are going to walk along the bank of the River Hayle, downstream, away from the church. Stay on the right-hand bank. The footpath leaves the back of the small car-park on the left of the bridge as you arrived along the road from the station. This is a permissive footpath and isn't marked on Ordnance Survey maps as a right of way.

Along the river, watch out for kingfishers which sometimes fly up and down here, particularly during winter. In summer you may see golden-ringed dragonflies and beautiful demoiselles (a type of damselfly). On the

A flooded section of Ryan's Field near the RSPB hide

right-hand side of this footpath is a pitch and putt course; here you may see green woodpeckers feeding on ants among the short grass. Always be on the look-out for grey wagtails. On the left-hand side of the river is some wet woodland, where there may be warblers; in the winter, occasional firecrests are seen here.

A little further along, just before the footpath passes under the A30, there is a sewage farm on the left where I have seen green sandpipers flying around. On the right is an area of reeds; look here for reed and sedge warblers in the summer.

Pass under the A30, and climb the bank to the right. The building resembling a bungalow is actually a birdwatching hide, owned by the RSPB. The RSPB owns the entire estuary as well as Ryan's Field (in front of the hide). 20 mins

There will be a few birds here, including maybe an odd grey heron and little egret, but it is only a busy spot for birds on excep-

The River Hayle and tidal sluice

tionally high tides. One of the problems with this field is that the ground has a high level of mine-related heavy metals, which prevent it becoming a useful place for birds to feed, so it is generally only used as a roosting area.

Continue along the river to the sluice gate; this is a relatively new sluice, opened in 2002 to help defend against flooding. At the main road, you will eventually turn right and walk along the footpath alongside the road, but before that there are two options.

1 *If it is June or early July, then it is worth turning left along the footpath and heading up towards the roundabout on the A30.*

Alongside this road you will see lots of wildflowers, including southern marsh, pyramidal and maybe bee orchids; yellow bartsia; common broomrape (often on the central reservation!); grass vetchling and others.

2 *At any time of year you must cross the main road (carefully) to view the main estuary.*

Here you will see wading birds and wild-

The view over the Hayle Estuary from The Causeway

fowl. Winter is the busiest time, with teal, wigeon, bar-tailed godwit, redshank, curlew, little egret, greenshank, dunlin, gulls and many more birds here. Spring and autumn are also very good for estuary birds, with less common species including little stint, curlew sandpiper, whimbrel, and often some very rare birds. In winter, peregrine falcons sometimes hunt over the estuary; look also for sparrowhawks, kestrels and buzzards.

Now head off on the footpath alongside The Causeway. Cross the minor road leading off to the right, and then cross over to the other side of the main road to stay on the footpath. After passing the factory on the left, and the 'Welcome to Hayle' sign, turn left (back left) on the footpath. 40 mins

This footpath goes around the edge of Carnsew Pool – a tidal pool – and returns to the same spot on the road. It allows excellent views of birds on the estuary. Simply follow the

Carnsew Pool (above left). Looking across to Lelant (above right). A view across Hayle harbour towards Copperhouse (left)

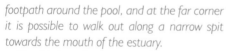

footpath around the pool, and at the far corner it is possible to walk out along a narrow spit towards the mouth of the estuary.

The birds to be seen on the estuary are similar to those already listed, but on the pool you may see a couple of different species. This is one of the best places in Cornwall to see great northern divers, during the winter, and little grebes occur here outside the breeding season. There may also be other divers and grebes, particularly after stormy weather. Around the harbour, look for cormorants standing on buoys and fishing in the river. Kingfishers may be seen anywhere round here in the winter, and keep an eye out for an odd osprey during late August and September.

After completing the circumnavigation of the pool, turn right on the main road, and head back from the direction in which you came. 1 hr 5 mins

This time, turn left on the minor road, and immediately cross the road and follow the small footpath that runs alongside the road. Where

The narrow spit which extends towards the mouth of the estuary

this footpath emerges on the road again, just before the railway bridge, turn right on to the track into the RSPB reserve car-park. This leads back to the birdwatching hide, and then the return route is back along the river on the same footpath. 1 hr 30 mins

12 Hayle to Godrevy

Beauty	*****
Wildlife	*****
Historical interest	****
General interest	****
Distance	15 km (10 miles)
Time	4½ hours
Walking conditions	Very easy
Timing	Must walk beach route approx 3 hours on either side of low tide
Start and end point	Car-park (free) at the swimming pool in Hayle SW 557 377, or a pay-and-display car-park at Hayle Towans SW 552 383
Get to to start point	From Copperhouse end of Hayle, head west along road through Hayle. Pass Copperhouse Pool on your right, and immediately turn right over single-track bridge. Soon turn right and park in swimming-pool car-park on right, or go straight on to pay-and-display car-park at Hayle Towans (bumpy road)
Note	Dogs not allowed on some parts of beach Easter to end Sept

A view to Godrevy from the beach near the mouth of the River Hayle

This is a beautiful walk with far-reaching views across St Ives Bay, and the lighthouse of Godrevy is always in view. There is a great spot for lunch in a café near the mouth of the Red River, and plenty of wildflowers and other wildlife along the way. This walk follows the coast path along the top of the towans (Cornish name for sand dunes) one way, and returns on the beach. The section along the beach cannot be undertaken at high tide, and it isn't safe to attempt it when the tide is rising near its peak. For this reason, you might need to do the walk in the opposite direction to that described here. Let the tide times determine your plans.

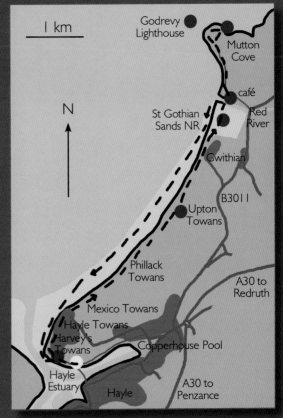

1 km

N

Godrevy
Lighthouse

Mutton
Cove

café

St Gothian
Sands NR

Red
River

Gwithian

B3011

Upton
Towans

A30 to
Redruth

Phillack
Towans

Mexico Towans

Hayle Towans

Harvey's
Towans

Copperhouse Pool

Hayle
Estuary

Hayle

A30 to
Penzance

The view from Hayle Towans across to St Ives

The car-park is adjacent to Copperhouse Pool, a RSPB reserve. This is great for bird life. Probably at its best in winter, with lots of waders and wildfowl (lapwing, redshank, dunlin, oystercatcher, wigeon, teal, etc.); but throughout the year look for little egret, shelduck, cormorant, etc. At times of passage, many rarer species occur here, including curlew, sandpiper, little stint and whimbrel to name but a few.

Leave the car-park with the swimming pool on your left, and walk along the road beside the old harbour. This road makes a slightly inauspicious beginning to this walk as it is used by lorries collecting sand from a depot a few hundred metres along here. Soon you will pass this depot

A caravan site at Mexico Towans (left). Part of the old dynamite works at Upton Towans (above)

and the site of the old power station, and the scenery will begin to mellow!

The power station here was coal fired, and was open between 1910 and 1977. It was supplied with coal from Wales which was brought in to the harbour.

Continue to follow the road-cum-track to the pay-and-display car-park at Harvey's Towans. From the car-park, head right on a track pass- ing chalets along the way. Soon the path meets a road; turn left here, and almost immediately left on to a footpath. This is the coast path, and you will follow it all the way to Godrevy Point. The route is well marked with posts showing the acorn symbol of the coast path. Where the gap between posts is too great to see the next one, generally look for the biggest track and don't head too far inland. It isn't possible to get too far lost! I will only give brief tips for certain parts of the route in the following text.

At Mexico Towans, there are refreshments available in season. The path narrows and goes to the left of the chalets of Beachside Leisure Park, soon passing a lifeguard shelter and entering Phillack Towans. After St Ives Bay Holiday Park, the path heads inland a little and soon enters Upton Towans. 50 mins

St Gothian Sands Nature Reserve is on the route

Upton Towans is now a nature reserve owned by Cornwall Wildlife Trust. However, from the late nineteenth to early twentieth century it was a dynamite factory. The coast path leads past at least one of the old buildings and along an old tramway. Around the building you can still see the embankment which was built around every processing building to deflect any possible explosion upwards rather than outwards. The tramways formed an extensive network of rail links between the different processes on site. To explore more of this area, head inland a little if you wish.

Now the towans are a nature reserve, and are particularly rich in flora. June and July are probably best for seeing flowers, with

There are several lakes at St Gothian Sands

pyramidal orchid, eyebright, storksbill, viper's bugloss and sea spurge all being common; in August look for autumn lady's tresses. Butterflies include silver-studded blue (June) and dark green fritillary (July to September); among the moths are six-spot burnet and garden tiger. Birds include stonechat, lots of skylarks, kestrel and meadow pipit.

After Upton Towans comes Gwithian Towans, where there is a big car-park, toilets and a couple of cafés. Continue a short distance to St Gothian Sands where the footpath heads inland slightly; follow the slate marker posts here. 1 hr 45 mins

This was once an area where sand was extracted, but fortunately now it is a nature

Godrevy lighthouse in a storm

reserve and the coast path crosses the middle of it. A couple of wetland areas have been formed, and these are great for birds, including sand martins in summer (these nest in cliffs at the mouth of the Red River), shelduck, waders, gulls, pipits and wagtails. Where the dunes drop down to the reserve, look for sea holly, which is very common here. In the gravel that forms the embankment alongside the river, there is a colony of rare mining bees.

The path leads through the reserve and crosses the Red River over a small bridge. The Sandsifter restaurant can be accessed to the right, or continue to the left and up the steps to a National Trust car-park and privately owned

café which I can thoroughly recommend for lunch. The route from here will continue as far as and then around Godrevy Point, and will return to this same car-park and café, so if you want to delay eating for an hour you can do.
2 hrs

Continue through the car-park and take the coast path to the left. This path leads to Godrevy Point.

Godrevy Lighthouse is one of the most iconic landmarks in Cornwall. It was the loss of the *Nile*, a 700-ton steamer with all her crew and passengers, in 1854 that led to the construction of the lighthouse. Building began in early 1858, and the 26 m-high tower was first illuminated in March 1859. In 1995, it was modernized, and is now powered by solar energy.

From the headland, look out to sea with binoculars and you may see bottlenose dolphins, porpoises, gannets, shearwaters, auks (razorbills and guillemots), fulmars and kittiwakes. Around the coast you might be lucky enough to spot a peregrine falcon. Shags nest on the sheer cliffs just a little way round the headland, but be very careful near the edge. Flowers growing here include spring squill, thrift, sea campion and kidney vetch.

Continue around the headland, and soon you will be able to look down into a cove,

Seals hauled out at Mutton Cove

known as Mutton Cove. Here, so long as it isn't high tide, you should be able to see grey seals. They have a breeding colony here and are present in some numbers throughout the year. Do not attempt to descend down into this cove; you will disturb the seals and endanger your life.

The beach at Gwithian

Turn right here, and head down towards the coast path to make the return to the National Trust car-park previously mentioned. 3 hrs

Head back down to the small bridge that you crossed on the way, but now turn right along the edge of the river and on to the beach. If you have timed your walk well, the tide will be out and you will be able to see three miles of beautiful golden sand stretching out in front of you.

The beach is very popular for various outdoor activities, from surfing and kite-surfing to sand-yachting. Wading birds using the beach here include sanderling, particularly from late summer to winter.

The cliffs around Gwithian reach a height of 20 m, and a range of coastal erosion features can be seen here, including stacks and caves. The rocks forming the cliffs are sedimentary,